Cooking Light®

TEX-MEX

Also in the Cooking Light® series

BREADS, GRAINS & PASTAS
DESSERTS
FISH & SHELLFISH
MICROWAVE
POULTRY
SALADS & DRESSINGS

Cooking Light®

TEX-MEX

80 Tasty and Tangy Recipes for Enchiladas and Ensaladas, Tacos and Tortillas, Fajitas and Flan, and Much More

WARNER BOOKS

A Time Warner Company

PHOTOGRAPHER: *Jim Bathie*

PHOTO STYLIST: *Kay E. Clarke*

BOOK DESIGN: *Giorgetta Bell McRee*

COVER DESIGN: *Andrew Newman*

Warner Books, Inc., 1271 Avenue of the Americas, New York, NY 10020

W A Time Warner Company

Printed in the United States of America
First printing: July 1992
10 9 8 7 6 5 4 3 2 1

Library of Congress Cataloging-in-Publication Data

Cooking light Tex-Mex : 80 tasty and tangy recipes for enchiladas and
ensaladas, tacos and tortillas, fajitas and flan, and much more!
    p.   cm.
Includes index.
ISBN 0-446-39404-1
1. Mexican American cookery.
TX715.2.S69C66   1992
641.5972—dc20

91-35920
CIP

CONTENTS

EATING WELL IS
THE BEST REWARD

Welcome to Cooking Light, a cookbook that celebrates the pleasures of good health. These low-fat, low-calorie recipes are easy to make, a delight to behold, and a feast for the senses.

Guided by the belief that good health and good food are synonymous, Cooking Light provides an approach to eating and cooking that is both healthy and appealing. Using the eighty recipes in this book, you will see how easy it is to minimize fat and sodium while maximizing minerals, fiber, and vitamins. And you will be delighted by the emphasis on the good taste and texture of fresh wholesome food cooked the light way.

So eat hearty, slim down and delight yourself, your family, and your friends with these easy-to-prepare, all-natural, and very delicious recipes.

EDITOR'S NOTE

Unless otherwise indicated:

eggs are large

margarine is corn oil margarine

sugar is granulated white sugar

flour is all-purpose

raisins are "dark"

cranberries and other ingredients are fresh

prepared mustard is regular store-bought yellow mustard

chicken breast is cooked without skin and without salt

vinegar is regular distilled vinegar

Cooking Light.

TEX-MEX

DRINKS

KAHLÚA CIDER

3 cups unsweetened apple cider
2 tablespoons Kahlúa or other coffee-flavored liqueur
4 (3-inch) cinnamon sticks

Place apple cider in a large saucepan; bring to a boil over medium heat. Remove from heat, and stir in Kahlúa. Pour cider into mugs; stir each serving with a cinnamon stick. Serve immediately. Yield: 3 cups (110 calories per ¾-cup serving).

PROTEIN 0.1 / FAT 0.2 / CARBOHYDRATE 23.8 / CHOLESTEROL 0 / IRON 0.7 / SODIUM 6 / CALCIUM 13

FROZEN PIÑA COLADA

4 cups chopped fresh pineapple
1 teaspoon grated orange rind
½ cup unsweetened orange juice
3 tablespoons skim milk
3 tablespoons light rum
1 tablespoon plus 1½ teaspoons lemon juice
½ teaspoon coconut extract

Combine all ingredients in container of an electric blender, and process until smooth. Transfer mixture to a 9-inch metal pan. Freeze 3 hours or until almost frozen.

Place frozen mixture in container of an electric blender; process until smooth. Return mixture to metal pan. Freeze again until firm. Spoon into glasses, and serve immediately. Yield: 8 servings (54 calories per ½-cup serving).

PROTEIN 0.6 / FAT 0.4 / CARBOHYDRATE 11.9 / FIBER 1.2 / CHOLESTEROL 0 / SODIUM 4 / POTASSIUM 130

LIME SANGRÍA

4 cups dry white wine, chilled
1½ cups club soda, chilled
¼ cup Cognac
¼ cup Triple Sec or other orange-flavored liqueur
¼ cup lime juice
3 tablespoons sugar
1 orange, thinly sliced
1 lime, thinly sliced

Combine first 6 ingredients, stirring until sugar dissolves. Pour over crushed ice in serving glasses, and garnish with orange and lime slices. Yield: 6 cups (187 calories per ¾-cup serving).

PROTEIN 0.2 / FAT 0.0 / CARBOHYDRATE 11.0 / FIBER 0.0 / CHOLESTEROL 0 / SODIUM 6 / POTASSIUM 107

MOCK SANGRÍA

---

1 (25.4-ounce) bottle sparkling pink Catawba, chilled
3 cups cranapple juice, chilled
3 tablespoons lime juice, chilled
1 tablespoon instant powdered tea
1 (10-ounce) bottle club soda, chilled
Orange slices
Lime slices
Lemon slices

Combine first 5 ingredients in a serving pitcher just before serving; stir until well blended. Float orange, lime, and lemon slices in pitcher to garnish. Pour over ice in serving glasses, and serve immediately. Yield: 8 cups (116 calories per 1-cup serving).

PROTEIN 0.4 / FAT 0.1 / CARBOHYDRATE 29.3 / FIBER 0.1 / CHOLESTEROL 0 / SODIUM 7 / POTASSIUM 207

APPETIZERS

QUESADILLAS

---

4 (8-inch) flour tortillas
¾ cup (3 ounces) reduced-fat Monterey Jack cheese
¼ cup commercial salsa

Place 2 tortillas on an ungreased baking sheet. Sprinkle evenly with cheese. Spoon 2 tablespoons salsa onto each tortilla. Top with remaining tortillas. Bake tortillas at 450° for 4 minutes on each side. To serve, cut each tortilla into 8 wedges. Yield: 16 wedges (49 calories per wedge).

PROTEIN 2.3 / FAT 1.7 / CARBOHYDRATE 6.8 / CHOLESTEROL 4 / IRON 0.3 / SODIUM 34 / CALCIUM 51

TORTILLA ROLL-UPS

¼ cup light process cream cheese product
2 tablespoons no-sugar-added apricot spread
1 tablespoon crunchy peanut butter
2 teaspoons skim milk
6 (6-inch) flour tortillas, softened

Combine first 4 ingredients; stir well. Spread 1 tablespoon plus 1½ teaspoons cream cheese mixture evenly over each tortilla. Roll up jelly roll fashion. Wrap each tortilla roll in plastic wrap, and chill at least 2 hours. To serve, slice into 1-inch pieces. Yield: 3 dozen (22 calories each).

PROTEIN 0.6 / FAT 0.8 / CARBOHYDRATE 3.5 / CHOLESTEROL 0 / IRON 0.1 / SODIUM 12 / CALCIUM 6

HOT MEXICAN-STYLE BROCCOLI DIP

1 (10-ounce) package frozen chopped broccoli, thawed
Vegetable cooking spray
½ cup chopped onion
1¼ cups peeled, seeded, and chopped tomato
2 tablespoons chopped jalapeño pepper
1 (8-ounce) package Neufchâtel cheese, cubed and softened
1 cup (4 ounces) shredded reduced-fat Monterey Jack cheese
¾ cup evaporated skim milk
⅓ cup sliced ripe olives

Drain broccoli; press between paper towels to remove excess moisture. Place broccoli in container of an electric blender or food processor; process until smooth. Set mixture aside.

Coat a large nonstick skillet with cooking spray; place over medium-high heat until hot. Add onion, and sauté until tender. Add tomato and jalapeño pepper; sauté 2 minutes. Transfer mixture to a large bowl. Stir in reserved broccoli, cheeses, milk, and olives. Spoon into a 1½-quart casserole coated with cooking spray. Bake at 400° for 50 minutes or until bubbly and browned. Serve warm with unsalted tortilla chips or melba rounds. Yield: 4½ cups (18 calories per tablespoon).

PROTEIN 1.1 / FAT 1.2 / CARBOHYDRATE 0.9 / CHOLESTEROL 4 / IRON 0.1 / SODIUM 31 / CALCIUM 14

TEQUILA DIP WITH JICAMA CHIPS

¾ cup plus 1 tablespoon low-fat sour cream
¾ cup plain nonfat yogurt
2 tablespoons tequila
1 tablespoon chili powder
½ teaspoon grated lime rind
¼ teaspoon hot sauce
1 (2-pound) jicama, peeled and cut into ¼-inch slices

Combine first 6 ingredients; stir well. Cover and chill. Cut jicama into rounds, using a 2-inch cookie cutter. Serve with tequila dip. Yield: 1¾ cups dip plus 4 dozen jicama chips (24 calories per tablespoon dip and 2 jicama chips).

PROTEIN 0.8 / FAT 0.9 / CARBOHYDRATE 2.6 / CHOLESTEROL 3 / IRON 0.2 / SODIUM 12 / CALCIUM 23

MEXICAN PIZZA SNACKS

2 (8-inch) flour tortillas
½ (1-pound) package frozen raw ground turkey, thawed
⅓ cup chopped onion
½ (8-ounce) can no-salt-added tomato sauce
1 (4-ounce) can chopped green chiles, undrained
1¼ teaspoons chili powder
½ teaspoon ground cumin
¾ cup chopped tomato
¾ cup (3 ounces) shredded part-skim mozzarella cheese

Place tortillas on an ungreased baking sheet. Bake at 350° for 4 to 5 minutes or until crisp. Set tortillas aside.

Cook turkey and onion in a large nonstick skillet over medium heat until turkey is browned, stirring to crumble. Drain and pat dry with paper towels. Wipe pan drippings from skillet with a paper towel. Return turkey mixture to skillet. Stir in tomato sauce, green chiles, chili powder, and cumin. Cook over medium heat until mixture is thoroughly heated. Spoon ¾ cup turkey mixture over each tortilla. Sprinkle chopped tomato and cheese evenly over turkey mixture. Broil 4 to 6 inches from heat for 1 minute or until cheese melts. To serve, cut each tortilla into 6 wedges. Yield: 12 servings (75 calories per serving).

PROTEIN 6.8 / FAT 2.4 / CARBOHYDRATE 7.1 / CHOLESTEROL 15 / IRON 0.6 / SODIUM 49 / CALCIUM 59

NACHOS

24 unsalted tortilla chips (about 2 ounces)
Vegetable cooking spray
½ cup (2 ounces) shredded part-skim farmer's cheese
3 tablespoons plus 1½ teaspoons chopped green chiles

Spread a single layer of tortilla chips in a jelly roll pan coated with cooking spray. Sprinkle with cheese and chiles. Bake at 350° for 5 minutes or until cheese melts. Yield: 2 dozen appetizers. Serving size: 1 nacho (20 calories each).

PROTEIN 0.8 / FAT 1.3 / CARBOHYDRATE 1.5 / FIBER 0.0 / CHOLESTEROL 2 / SODIUM 53 / POTASSIUM 7

FRESH CORN RELISH DIP

1 cup fresh corn
3 ounces Neufchâtel cheese, softened
2 tablespoons low-fat sour cream
1 tablespoon reduced-calorie mayonnaise
1 tablespoon lime juice
2 tablespoons finely chopped sweet red pepper
2 tablespoons finely chopped green onions
1 tablespoon minced fresh cilantro
1 teaspoon chopped jalapeño pepper
Fresh corn husks (optional)
Sweet red pepper ring (optional)
Fresh parsley sprigs (optional)

Cook corn in a small amount of water until tender. Drain. Mash gently with a fork; set aside.

Combine Neufchâtel cheese, sour cream, mayonnaise, and lime juice in a small bowl. Beat at medium speed of an electric mixer until smooth. Stir in red pepper, green onions, cilantro, jalapeño pepper, and reserved corn. Chill.

Serve dip in corn husks, if desired, with raw vegetables or unsalted tortilla chips. If desired, garnish with pepper ring and parsley sprigs. Yield: 1½ cups (19 calories per tablespoon).

PROTEIN 0.6 / FAT 1.2 / CARBOHYDRATE 1.6 / CHOLESTEROL 3 / IRON 0.1 / SODIUM 20 / CALCIUM 5

SPICY TORTILLA CHIPS

3 tablespoons vegetable oil
1 tablespoon water
3 cloves garlic
½ teaspoon dried whole oregano
½ teaspoon ground cumin
¼ teaspoon paprika
⅛ teaspoon salt
⅛ teaspoon pepper
⅛ teaspoon ground red pepper
1 (8-ounce) package 8-inch corn tortillas

Combine first 9 ingredients in container of an electric blender, and process 1 to 2 minutes or until pureed. Brush both sides of tortillas with mixture; stack tortillas, and cut into 8 wedges. Arrange wedges in a single layer in jelly roll pans, and bake at 400° for 10 minutes or until crisp and lightly browned. Serve warm or store in airtight containers. Yield: 8 dozen appetizers. Serving size: 1 chip (13 calories each).

PROTEIN 0.2 / FAT 0.5 / CARBOHYDRATE 1.8 / FIBER 0.0 / CHOLESTEROL 0 / SODIUM 6 / POTASSIUM 1

PICO DE GALLO WITH CHIPS

3 medium tomatoes, peeled and finely chopped
2 green onions, finely chopped
1 (4-ounce) can chopped green chiles, drained
2 tablespoons chopped fresh cilantro
1 tablespoon chopped jalapeño pepper
1 teaspoon vinegar
1 teaspoon vegetable oil
Crispy Chips

Combine all ingredients except Crispy Chips in a medium bowl; mix well. Cover and chill thoroughly. Serve with Crispy Chips. Yield: 3 cups. Serving size: 1 chip plus 2 teaspoons sauce (17 calories per serving).

Crispy Chips:

8 (6-inch) corn tortillas
2 teaspoons vegetable oil
1 teaspoon chili powder

Lightly brush one side of each tortilla with oil; sprinkle with chili powder. Stack tortillas, and cut into 8 wedges. Arrange wedges in a single layer on baking sheets; bake at 400° for 10 minutes or until wedges are crisp and lightly browned. Serve warm or cool. Store in an airtight container. Yield: 64 chips.

PROTEIN 0.5 / FAT 0.4 / CARBOHYDRATE 3.1 / FIBER 0.1 / CHOLESTEROL 0 / SODIUM 13 / POTASSIUM 17

MEXICAN NIBBLES

1 egg white
2½ teaspoons chili powder
½ teaspoon ground cumin
¼ teaspoon garlic powder
3 cups bite-size crispy corn squares cereal
Vegetable cooking spray

Beat egg white (at room temperature) in a large bowl until foamy. Combine next 3 ingredients in a small bowl; stir well, and fold into egg white. Add cereal; stir gently to coat pieces evenly. Spread cereal mixture on a baking sheet coated with cooking spray. Bake at 325° for 15 minutes, stirring every 5 minutes. Let cereal mixture cool on baking sheet; store in an airtight container. Yield: 6 cups. Serving size: ½ cup (63 calories per serving).

PROTEIN 1.7 / FAT 0.3 / CARBOHYDRATE 13.2 / FIBER 0.5 / CHOLESTEROL 0 / SODIUM 155 / POTASSIUM 43

GRILLED QUESADILLAS WITH YOGURT SALSA

½ cup (2 ounces) shredded Monterey Jack cheese
½ cup (2 ounces) shredded Colby cheese
4 (8-inch) flour tortillas
1 tablespoon plus 1 teaspoon chopped green chiles
Vegetable cooking spray
Yogurt Salsa

Sprinkle 2 tablespoons each Monterey Jack and Colby cheese just off center of each tortilla. Top each with 1 teaspoon green chiles. Arrange tortillas on a grill coated with cooking spray. Grill 6 inches over hot coals 1 minute or until undersides of tortillas are golden brown. Fold in half; grill 30 seconds or until cheese melts. Cut each tortilla into 4 wedges. Top each wedge with Yogurt Salsa, and serve immediately. Yield: 16 appetizers. Serving size: 1 quesadilla plus 1½ teaspoons salsa (64 calories each).

Yogurt Salsa:

¼ cup plain low-fat yogurt
2 tablespoons chopped tomato
1 tablespoon chopped onion
2 teaspoons minced fresh cilantro
½ teaspoon lemon juice
¼ teaspoon salt

Combine yogurt, tomato, onion, cilantro, lemon juice, and salt in a small bowl; stir well. Cover and chill 2 hours. Yield: ½ cup.

PROTEIN 2.7 / FAT 3.0 / CARBOHYDRATE 7.4 / CHOLESTEROL 6 / IRON 0.3 / SODIUM 97 / CALCIUM 67

MINI-CHICKEN TOSTADAS

1 cup finely chopped, cooked chicken breast (skinned
  before cooking and cooked without salt)
½ cup chopped, peeled jicama
1 (4-ounce) can chopped green chiles, drained
½ cup (2 ounces) shredded Cheddar cheese
3 tablespoons reduced-calorie mayonnaise
12 (6-inch) corn tortillas

Combine chicken and next 4 ingredients in a small bowl; stir well. Set aside.

    Cut each tortilla into 3 circles using a 2-inch biscuit cutter. Place tortilla chips on an ungreased baking sheet. Bake at 350° for 5 minutes. Spread 1 tablespoon of reserved chicken mixture on each tortilla chip. Broil 4 to 5 inches from heating element 3 minutes or until hot and bubbly. Yield: 3 dozen appetizers. Serving size: 1 tostada (40 calories per serving).

PROTEIN 2.3 / FAT 1.4 / CARBOHYDRATE 4.6 / CHOLESTEROL 5 / IRON 0.5 / SODIUM 42 / CALCIUM 26

RIO GRANDE SALSA WITH TORTILLA CHIPS

3 small tomatoes, peeled, seeded, and chopped
1 small green pepper, seeded and chopped
1 small purple onion, chopped
1 medium jalapeño pepper, seeded and chopped
1 clove garlic, minced
1 tablespoon chopped fresh cilantro
1½ teaspoons red wine vinegar
⅛ teaspoon salt
48 plain tortilla chips

Combine tomatoes, green pepper, purple onion, jalapeño pepper, garlic, chopped cilantro, red wine vinegar, and salt in a medium bowl, stirring until well blended. Cover and chill thoroughly. Serve salsa with tortilla chips. Yield: 3 cups. Serving size: ¼ cup salsa plus 4 tortilla chips (65 calories per serving).

PROTEIN 1.3 / FAT 3.0 / CARBOHYDRATE 8.8 / CHOLESTEROL 0 / IRON 0.6 / SODIUM 35 / CALCIUM 8

PEPPY MEXICAN POPCORN

⅔ cup unpopped popcorn
1 tablespoon vegetable oil
1 tablespoon plus 1½ teaspoons margarine, melted
1 teaspoon chili powder
1 teaspoon paprika
⅛ teaspoon red pepper
⅛ teaspoon garlic powder

Combine popcorn and oil in a Dutch oven; cover and cook over medium-high heat 2 minutes or until popped, shaking pan after corn starts to pop. Place popcorn in bowl; set aside.

Combine margarine and remaining ingredients. Toss with reserved popcorn in bowl. Yield: 8 cups. Serving size: 1 cup (98 calories per serving).

PROTEIN 2.1 / FAT 4.7 / CARBOHYDRATE 12.7 / CHOLESTEROL 0 / IRON 0.5 / SODIUM 29 / CALCIUM 4

GREEN CHILE-CORN DIP

1 (8-ounce) carton 1% low-fat cottage cheese
½ cup frozen whole kernel corn, thawed
2 tablespoons commercial picante sauce
⅛ teaspoon garlic powder
⅛ teaspoon ground cumin
2 tablespoons canned chopped green chiles, drained
1 tablespoon diced sweet red pepper
2 tablespoons frozen whole kernel corn, thawed

Combine first 5 ingredients in container of an electric blender; process until almost smooth. Gently fold in green chiles, red pepper, and 2 tablespoons corn. Cover dip, and chill at least 1 hour. Serve dip with fresh raw vegetables. Yield: 1½ cups (11 calories per tablespoon).

PROTEIN 1.3 / FAT 0.1 / CARBOHYDRATE 1.2 / CHOLESTEROL 0 / IRON 0.1 / SODIUM 49 / CALCIUM 6

SOUPS

MEXICAN LENTIL SOUP

Vegetable cooking spray
2¼ cups chopped onion
¾ cup chopped parsnips
½ cup chopped carrot
½ cup chopped celery
4 cups Spicy Vegetable Broth (recipe follows)
2 cups water
½ pound dried lentils
1 teaspoon ground cumin
1 teaspoon chili powder
1 (14½-ounce) can no-salt-added whole tomatoes,
    undrained and chopped
1 jalapeño pepper, seeded and chopped
¼ teaspoon hot sauce

Coat a large Dutch oven with cooking spray; place over medium-high heat until hot. Add chopped onion, and sauté 5 minutes or until tender.

Add parsnips and next 7 ingredients, stirring well. Bring vegetable mixture to a boil; cover, reduce heat, and simmer 30 minutes. Stir in tomatoes, chopped jalapeño pepper, and hot sauce; simmer an additional 45 minutes or until lentils are tender. To serve, ladle soup into individual bowls. Yield: 8 cups (141 calories per 1-cup serving).

PROTEIN 9.4 / FAT 0.7 / CARBOHYDRATE 26.0 / CHOLESTEROL 0 / IRON 3.8 / SODIUM 27 / CALCIUM 59

Spicy Vegetable Broth:

Vegetable cooking spray
3 cups peeled, diced turnips
1 cup diced carrot
1 cup diced onion
1 cup diced celery
1 cup diced sweet red pepper
6 cups water
2 cups spicy hot vegetable juice cocktail
¼ cup minced fresh parsley
2 teaspoons dried Italian seasoning
5 peppercorns
1 jalapeño pepper, seeded and diced
½ teaspoon ground red pepper

Coat a Dutch oven with cooking spray; place over medium-high heat until hot. Add turnips, carrot, onion, celery, and red pepper; sauté 15 minutes.

Stir in water and remaining ingredients. Bring to a boil. Cover, reduce heat, and simmer 2 hours. Strain broth through a double layer of cheesecloth; reserve vegetables for other uses. Cover and chill broth. Store in refrigerator or freezer. Use as a base for vegetable soups. Yield: 6 cups (24 calories per 1-cup serving).

PROTEIN 0.7 / FAT 0.2 / CARBOHYDRATE 4.8 / CHOLESTEROL 0 / IRON 1.1 / SODIUM 2 / CALCIUM 19

CHICKEN-TORTILLA SOUP

2 (8-inch) corn tortillas, cut into strips
Vegetable cooking spray
1 medium onion, chopped
1 cup diced tomato
1 clove garlic
¼ teaspoon dried whole oregano
1 quart water
2 teaspoons chicken-flavored bouillon granules
¾ pound chicken breast halves, skinned
1 cup diced tomato
½ medium avocado, peeled and cubed
½ cup (2 ounces) shredded sharp Cheddar cheese
2 teaspoons minced hot chile pepper

Place tortilla strips on a baking sheet coated with cooking spray, and bake at 350° for 10 to 15 minutes or until golden and crisp. Set aside.

Place onion, 1 cup tomato, garlic, and oregano in container of an electric blender, and process until pureed. Transfer puree to a large saucepan, and simmer 5 minutes, stirring constantly. Stir in water and bouillon granules, and bring to a boil. Reduce heat, and add chicken breasts; simmer 15 to 20 minutes or until chicken is done.

Remove chicken from soup, keeping soup warm. Let chicken cool to touch; bone and cut meat into cubes. Return chicken to soup. Cook over low heat until thoroughly heated.

Ladle soup into soup bowls. Divide tortilla strips, 1 cup tomato, avocado, cheese, and chile pepper among bowls, and serve immediately. Yield: 7 cups (135 calories per 1-cup serving).

PROTEIN 10.8 / FAT 6.2 / CARBOHYDRATE 9.7 / FIBER 1.0 / CHOLESTEROL 28 / SODIUM 189 / POTASSIUM 300

BLACK BEAN SOUP

1 (16-ounce) package dried black beans
9 cups water
2 cloves garlic, halved and crushed
1 teaspoon salt
2 tablespoons lemon juice
3 cloves garlic
1½ teaspoons ground cumin
½ teaspoon dried whole oregano
2 to 4 drops hot sauce
1 medium onion, finely chopped
1½ cups finely chopped green pepper
Marinated Rice

Sort and wash beans; place in a large Dutch oven. Cover with water 2 inches above beans; let soak overnight. Drain beans, and return to Dutch oven. Add 9 cups water, 2 cloves garlic, and salt; bring to a boil. Cover partially; reduce heat to medium-low, and cook 2 hours or until beans are tender, stirring occasionally.

Combine lemon juice, 3 cloves garlic, cumin, oregano, and hot sauce in a pestle; crush well. Add lemon juice mixture, onion, and green peppers to beans. Bring to a boil; reduce heat and simmer, partially covered, 30 to 45 minutes, stirring occasionally. Ladle into soup bowls; garnish each with 2 tablespoons Marinated Rice. Yield: 8 cups (236 calories per 1-cup serving).

Marinated Rice:

⅔ cup cooked brown rice (cooked without salt or fat)
⅓ cup finely chopped tomato
1 green onion, chopped
2 teaspoons lemon juice
1 teaspoon olive oil

Combine all ingredients in a bowl; mix well. Cover; chill at least 3 hours. Yield: 1 cup.

PROTEIN 13.8 / FAT 1.8 / CARBOHYDRATE 43.0 / FIBER 15.2 / CHOLESTEROL 0 / SODIUM 311 / POTASSIUM 727

TORTILLA SOUP

Vegetable cooking spray
½ cup chopped onion
1 (4-ounce) can chopped green chiles, undrained
2 cloves garlic, crushed
3¾ cups water
1½ cups tomato juice
1 medium tomato, peeled and chopped
1 teaspoon beef-flavored bouillon granules
1 teaspoon ground cumin
1 teaspoon chili powder
1 teaspoon Worcestershire sauce
¼ teaspoon pepper
2 to 4 drops hot sauce
3 (6-inch) corn tortillas, cut into ½-inch strips
½ cup (2 ounces) shredded Monterey Jack cheese
Fresh cilantro sprigs

Coat a small Dutch oven with cooking spray; place over medium heat until hot. Add onion, green chiles, and garlic, and cook until onion is tender, stirring frequently. Add water, tomato juice, tomato, bouillon granules, cumin, chili powder, Worcestershire sauce, pepper, and hot sauce; stir well. Bring to a boil. Cover; reduce heat, and simmer 1 hour. Add tortillas; cover and simmer 10 minutes.

Ladle hot soup into serving bowls. Sprinkle 1 tablespoon cheese over each, and garnish with a cilantro sprig. Yield: 8 cups (89 calories per 1-cup serving).

PROTEIN 3.6 / FAT 2.9 / CARBOHYDRATE 13.0 / FIBER 0.7 / CHOLESTEROL 6 / SODIUM 299 / POTASSIUM 265

SALADS

STIR-FRY FAJITA SALAD

1 pound beef flank steak
2 tablespoons lime juice
1 tablespoon vinegar
1½ teaspoons vegetable oil
⅛ teaspoon salt
¼ teaspoon pepper
1 clove garlic, sliced
1 tablespoon minced fresh cilantro
Vegetable cooking spray
1 tablespoon vegetable oil
1 medium-size sweet red pepper, sliced
2 medium-size green chiles, seeded and chopped
¾ cup sliced green onions
2 cups peeled, seeded, and chopped tomato
3 cups torn leaf lettuce
3 cups torn romaine lettuce

Trim excess fat from steak; place in a shallow dish. Combine lime juice and next 6 ingredients, stirring well; pour over steak. Cover and marinate in refrigerator 8 hours or overnight, turning occasionally.

Partially freeze steak; slice meat diagonally across grain into thin strips, and set aside.

Coat a wok or skillet with cooking spray; add oil. Allow to heat at medium-high (325°) for 2 minutes. Add red pepper, green chiles, and green onions; stir-fry 2 minutes. Remove vegetables from wok, and set aside.

Add half of reserved steak to wok; stir-fry 3 to 5 minutes; remove from wok, and repeat procedure with remaining steak.

Return reserved vegetables and steak to wok; add tomato, and stir-fry 1 minute. Remove wok from heat, and add lettuce, stirring constantly for 1 minute or until lettuce wilts. Serve immediately. Yield: 6 servings (192 calories per serving).

PROTEIN 16.9 / FAT 10.9 / CARBOHYDRATE 7.4 / CHOLESTEROL 38 / IRON 2.7 / SODIUM 115 / CALCIUM 29

MEXICAN DINNER SALAD

2 cups torn red leaf lettuce
2 cups torn romaine lettuce
1 cup cubed avocado
1 cup jicama, peeled and cut into ¼-inch strips
4 fresh tomatillos, husked and chopped
¼ cup tomato juice with green chiles
1 tablespoon red wine vinegar
2 teaspoons vegetable oil
¼ teaspoon sugar

Combine first 5 ingredients in a large bowl; set aside. Combine tomato juice, vinegar, oil, and sugar in a small bowl, mixing well. Pour dressing over salad, and toss well. Serve immediately. Yield: 6 servings (59 calories per serving).

PROTEIN 1.3 / FAT 4.2 / CARBOHYDRATE 4.8 / CHOLESTEROL 0 / IRON 0.6 / SODIUM 61 / CALCIUM 15

PINTO BEAN SALAD

2 (16-ounce) cans pinto beans
1 cup shredded Romaine lettuce
½ cup chopped celery
⅓ cup chopped purple onion
¼ cup chopped sweet red pepper
3 tablespoons red wine vinegar
2 tablespoons vegetable oil
2 teaspoons minced fresh cilantro
¼ teaspoon garlic salt
Lettuce leaves
½ cup (2 ounces) shredded Cheddar cheese

Place beans in a colander, and rinse under cold water 1 minute; set colander aside to let beans drain 1 minute.

Combine beans and next 4 ingredients in a large bowl; set aside. Combine vinegar, oil, cilantro, and garlic salt in a jar; cover tightly, and shake vigorously. Pour vinegar mixture over reserved bean mixture; toss gently to coat well. Cover and chill thoroughly.

To serve, spoon bean mixture into a lettuce-lined salad bowl; sprinkle with cheese. Yield: 8 servings (123 calories per serving).

PROTEIN 4.9 / FAT 6.3 / CARBOHYDRATE 11.7 / CHOLESTEROL 7 / IRON 0.9 / SODIUM 117 / CALCIUM 82

GUACAMOLE SALAD

1 (10-ounce) avocado, peeled and chopped
½ cup evaporated skim milk
3 tablespoons lemon juice
2 tablespoons sour cream
1 clove garlic, crushed
¼ teaspoon salt
¼ teaspoon chili powder
¼ teaspoon Worcestershire sauce

⅛ teaspoon ground cumin
2 drops hot sauce
1 (1-pound) head iceberg lettuce, shredded
¼ pound fresh spinach, shredded
1 (15-ounce) can garbanzo beans, drained
1 (14-ounce) can hearts of palm, drained and sliced
1 small red or green pepper, seeded and chopped

Combine first 10 ingredients in container of an electric blender; process until smooth.

Combine lettuce, spinach, garbanzo beans, and hearts of palm in a large salad bowl; toss lightly. Spoon onto individual salad plates. Top evenly with avocado mixture, and garnish with red or green pepper. Yield: 8 servings (150 calories per serving).

PROTEIN 5.5 / FAT 7.4 / CARBOHYDRATE 19.6 / FIBER 5.2 / CHOLESTEROL 2 / SODIUM 307 / POTASSIUM 675

SOUTHWESTERN JICAMA SALAD

½ cup vinegar
1 tablespoon plus 2 teaspoons sugar
1 tablespoon minced fresh cilantro
⅛ teaspoon salt
⅛ teaspoon pepper
Dash of hot sauce
2 cups shredded jicama
4 small tomatoes, sliced
2 fresh tomatillos, husked and sliced

Combine first 6 ingredients in a medium bowl; stir with a wire whisk until well blended. Add jicama, and toss gently.

Arrange tomato slices and tomatillo slices on individual salad plates, and top with ⅓ cup jicama mixture. Yield: 6 servings (57 calories per serving).

PROTEIN 1.7 / FAT 0.3 / CARBOHYDRATE 13.7 / CHOLESTEROL 0 / IRON 0.9 / SODIUM 62 / CALCIUM 16

ENSALADA TOSTADA

4 (4-ounce) skinned, boned chicken breast halves
2 bay leaves
¼ teaspoon salt
¼ teaspoon cracked pepper
6 (6-inch) corn tortillas
Vegetable cooking spray
2 heads romaine lettuce, torn into bite-size pieces
1 large avocado, cut into ½-inch cubes
1 large green pepper, diced
¾ cup chopped tomato
1 small purple onion, thinly sliced
⅓ cup chopped fresh cilantro
Dressing
Fresh cilantro sprigs (optional)

Place chicken in a large nonstick skillet; cover with cold water. Add bay leaves, salt, and cracked pepper. Bring to a boil over high heat; cover, reduce heat, and simmer 15 minutes or until done. Remove and discard bay leaves. Drain chicken and set aside.

Cut each tortilla into 8 wedges; place on a baking sheet that has been coated with cooking spray. Bake at 350° for 15 minutes or until crisp, turning once. Set aside.

Shred chicken into bite-size pieces. Combine chicken, lettuce, and next 5 ingredients in a large bowl. Pour ½ cup dressing over salad, and toss well. Garnish with cilantro sprigs, if desired. Serve with tortilla wedges and remaining ¾ cup dressing. Yield: 6 servings (241 calories per 3-cup serving).

Dressing:

⅓ cup hot water
¾ teaspoon chicken-flavored bouillon granules
⅓ cup water
¼ cup cider vinegar
2 tablespoons tarragon vinegar

1 tablespoon olive oil
1 teaspoon sugar
½ teaspoon kosher salt
1 teaspoon mustard seeds
1 teaspoon dry mustard
1 teaspoon paprika
¼ teaspoon pepper

Combine hot water and bouillon granules, stirring until granules dissolve. Combine bouillon mixture, ⅓ cup water, and remaining ingredients in a small bowl, stirring well with a wire whisk. Yield: 1¼ cups.

PROTEIN 21.7 / FAT 10.1 / CARBOHYDRATE 17.5 / CHOLESTEROL 47 / IRON 3.9 / SODIUM 482 / CALCIUM 94

EASY ENSALADA

5 cups torn salad greens
½ cup chopped zucchini
½ cup frozen whole kernel corn, thawed and drained
½ cup diced sweet red pepper
¼ cup sliced green onions
½ cup commercial reduced-calorie creamy cucumber
    dressing
¼ cup commercial picante sauce

Combine first 5 ingredients in a large bowl, tossing gently; chill.
   Combine dressing and picante sauce, stirring well. Cover dressing mixture and chill. To serve pour dressing over salad mixture; toss gently to combine. Yield: 6 servings (60 calories per ½-cup serving).

PROTEIN 1.3 / FAT 3.0 / CARBOHYDRATE 7.0 / CHOLESTEROL 0 / IRON 0.8 / SODIUM 369 / CALCIUM 24

MAIN DISHES

CHILES RELLEÑOS CASSEROLE

2 (4-ounce) cans chopped green chiles, drained
1 cup (4 ounces) shredded Monterey Jack cheese
½ cup (2 ounces) shredded sharp Cheddar cheese
Vegetable cooking spray
4 eggs, separated
¼ cup skim milk
1 tablespoon all-purpose flour
⅛ teaspoon pepper
Seasoned Tomato Sauce (recipe follows)

Layer green chiles and cheese in a 2-quart casserole coated with cooking spray. Set aside.

Combine yolks, milk, flour, and pepper; beat until well blended. Beat egg whites (at room temperature) until stiff peaks form; fold into yolks. Pour over cheese. Bake at 350° for 25 minutes or until puffed and golden brown. Spoon 2 tablespoons sauce over each serving. Yield: 6 servings (192 calories per serving).

Seasoned Tomato Sauce:

Vegetable cooking spray
¼ cup chopped green onion
1 clove garlic, minced
1 (8-ounce) can no-salt-added tomato sauce
¼ teaspoon chili powder
¼ teaspoon dried whole oregano
Dash of hot sauce

Coat a skillet with cooking spray; place over medium heat until hot. Add green onion and garlic; sauté until tender. Stir in remaining ingredients; cover and simmer 10 minutes. Yield: ¾ cup.

PROTEIN 12.1 / FAT 12.6 / CARBOHYDRATE 6.9 / FIBER 0.7 / CHOLESTEROL 208 / SODIUM 251 / POTASSIUM 302

HUEVOS RANCHEROS

Vegetable cooking spray
1 teaspoon vegetable oil
1 medium onion, chopped
2 medium-size green peppers, seeded and chopped
1 clove garlic, minced
1 (28-ounce) can whole tomatoes, drained and chopped
1 tablespoon minced fresh parsley
½ teaspoon minced green chiles
5 eggs
5 (8-inch) corn tortillas

Coat a skillet with cooking spray; add oil, and place over low heat until hot. Add onion, green pepper, and garlic; sauté until tender. Stir in tomatoes, parsley, and green chiles. Cover and simmer 15 minutes, stirring occasionally.

   Make 5 depressions in tomato sauce with the back of a spoon. Break 1 egg into each depression. Cover; cook over medium heat

1 minute. Spoon sauce over egg whites; cook 4 minutes or until desired degree of doneness.

While eggs are cooking, place tortillas on a baking sheet. Bake at 350° for 10 minutes or until crisp and golden. Place tortillas on serving plates. Remove eggs with a spatula, placing 1 egg on each tortilla. Cover eggs with sauce. Yield: 5 servings (236 calories per serving).

PROTEIN 10.8 / FAT 8.2 / CARBOHYDRATE 31.8 / FIBER 8.4 / CHOLESTEROL 274 / SODIUM 277 / POTASSIUM 428

NEW MEXICO OVEN OMELET

1 tablespoon cornstarch
¼ teaspoon salt
¼ teaspoon pepper
½ cup skim milk
4 eggs, separated
Vegetable cooking spray
¼ teaspoon cream of tartar
1 (8½-ounce) can whole kernel corn, drained
1 cup (4 ounces) shredded Colby cheese
1 (8-ounce) can no-salt-added tomato sauce
2 tablespoons drained chopped green chiles
4 drops hot sauce

Combine first 4 ingredients in a small saucepan; bring to a boil. Reduce heat, and cook, stirring frequently, until mixture thickens. Remove from heat, and set aside.

Beat egg yolks at high speed of an electric mixer 5 minutes or until thick and lemon colored. Add cornstarch mixture, beating well.

Place a 10-inch ovenproof skillet coated with cooking spray in a 350° oven for 4 minutes.

Beat egg whites (at room temperature) until foamy; add cream of tartar, and beat until stiff peaks form. Fold into yolk mixture, then gently fold in corn. Pour into heated skillet, and bake at 350°

for 20 minutes or until puffed and browned. Sprinkle with cheese, and bake 1 minute or until cheese melts.

Combine tomato sauce, green chiles, and hot sauce in a small saucepan. Cook over medium heat, stirring frequently, until thoroughly heated.

Cut omelet into 6 wedges and top with 2 tablespoons sauce; serve immediately. Yield: 6 servings (189 calories per serving).

PROTEIN 10.7 / FAT 10.2 / CARBOHYDRATE 14.6 / CHOLESTEROL 201 / IRON 1.1 / SODIUM 297 / CALCIUM 175

FIESTA EGG SCRAMBLE

Vegetable cooking spray
⅓ cup chopped sweet red pepper
3 tablespoons chopped green onions
2 tablespoons chopped green chiles, drained
1¼ cups frozen egg substitute with cheese, thawed
3 tablespoons skim milk
¼ cup (1 ounce) shredded reduced-fat Monterey Jack
   cheese
½ cup low-sodium picante sauce

Coat a large nonstick skillet with cooking spray; place over medium-high heat until hot. Add red pepper, green onions, and green chiles; sauté until vegetables are tender. Combine egg substitute and milk; stir well. Pour over pepper mixture in skillet, and cook over medium heat, stirring frequently, until egg substitute mixture is firm but still moist.

Remove from heat. Sprinkle cheese over eggs; cover and let stand 1 minute. Divide eggs evenly among 4 plates. Spoon 2 tablespoons picante sauce over each serving. Yield: 4 servings (123 calories per serving).

PROTEIN 11.8 / FAT 5.5 / CARBOHYDRATE 5.8 / CHOLESTEROL 8 / IRON 0.5 / SODIUM 387 / CALCIUM 79

BEEFY-TORTILLA PIE

Vegetable cooking spray
5 (6-inch) flour tortillas
½ pound ground chuck
1 (4-ounce) can chopped green chiles, drained
1 small onion, chopped
½ cup (2 ounces) shredded 40% less-fat Cheddar cheese
3 eggs, beaten
½ cup skim milk
3 tablespoons all-purpose flour
½ teaspoon baking powder
½ teaspoon chili powder
Jalapeño pepper flowers (optional)
Fresh cilantro sprigs (optional)

Coat bottom and sides of a 9-inch pieplate with cooking spray and line with tortillas. Set aside.

Cook ground chuck in a large nonstick skillet over medium heat until browned, stirring to crumble. Drain and pat dry with paper towels. Combine meat, green chiles, onion, and cheese; stir well. Spoon mixture into prepared dish.

Combine eggs and remaining ingredients in a large bowl; beat with a wire whisk until well blended. Pour egg mixture over beef mixture. Bake at 350° for 45 minutes or until set. If desired, garnish with jalapeño pepper flowers and fresh cilantro sprigs. Yield: 6 servings (268 calories per serving).

PROTEIN 15.8 / FAT 11.8 / CARBOHYDRATE 25.3 / CHOLESTEROL 160 / IRON 2.0 / SODIUM 170 / CALCIUM 160

TORTILLA TORTE

1 (15-ounce) can pinto beans
Vegetable cooking spray
½ cup chopped onion
1 clove garlic, minced
¼ teaspoon ground cumin
¼ cup commercial picante sauce
1 (4-ounce) can chopped green chiles, drained
4 (8-inch) whole wheat flour tortillas
¾ cup (3 ounces) shredded Monterey Jack cheese
2 tablespoons sliced ripe olives
2 cups shredded lettuce
1 medium tomato, chopped
Hot green pepper slices (optional)

Place pinto beans in a colander, and rinse under cold tap water 1 minute; set colander aside to let beans drain 1 minute.

Coat a large skillet with cooking spray; place over medium heat until hot. Add onion and garlic to skillet; sauté until tender. Stir in reserved pinto beans and cumin; reduce heat. Cook, uncovered, 30 minutes or until mixture is a thick paste, stirring occasionally and mashing beans with a wooden spoon. Set mixture aside, and keep warm.

Combine picante sauce and green chiles, and set aside.

Wrap tortillas in aluminum foil, and bake at 350° for 10 minutes or until thoroughly heated.

Place a tortilla on a baking sheet lightly coated with cooking spray. Top with one-third of bean mixture, one-third of picante sauce mixture, ¼ cup cheese, and 2 teaspoons olives. Repeat layers twice; top with remaining tortilla. Cover with foil, and bake at 350° for 15 minutes or until thoroughly heated. Transfer to a serving platter. Arrange shredded lettuce around torte. Top lettuce with chopped tomato, and garnish with hot green pepper slices, if desired. Cut into wedges to serve. Yield: 4 servings (269 calories per serving).

PROTEIN 13.0 / FAT 8.7 / CARBOHYDRATE 36.5 / FIBER 10.3 / CHOLESTEROL 17 / SODIUM 409 / POTASSIUM 462

BLACK BEAN–STUFFED TORTILLAS

1 (15-ounce) can black beans
Vegetable cooking spray
1 small onion, finely chopped
1 clove garlic, minced
1 teaspoon lime juice
¼ teaspoon dried whole oregano
¼ cup low-fat sour cream
2 teaspoons minced fresh cilantro
4 (6-inch) corn tortillas
1 (8-ounce) can no-salt-added tomato sauce
1 cup (4 ounces) shredded Monterey Jack cheese with
   jalapeño peppers

Place black beans in a colander, and rinse under cold tap water 1 minute; set colander aside to let beans drain 1 minute. Mash half of beans with a wooden spoon; set aside.

Coat a large skillet with cooking spray; place over medium heat until hot. Add onion and garlic; sauté until tender. Remove from heat, and stir in reserved beans, lime juice, and oregano; set aside. Combine sour cream and cilantro in a small bowl; stir well, and set aside.

Wrap tortillas in aluminum foil; bake at 325° for 10 minutes or until thoroughly heated. Spread 1 tablespoon reserved sour cream mixture on each tortilla. Spread reserved bean mixture evenly over tortillas, and fold in half.

Spread ⅓ cup tomato sauce in a 10- × 6- × 2-inch baking dish coated with cooking spray. Arrange folded tortillas over sauce. Top with remaining tomato sauce. Cover and bake at 350° for 15 minutes. Uncover, and sprinkle with shredded cheese. Bake an additional 5 minutes or until cheese melts. Yield: 4 servings (279 calories per serving).

PROTEIN 14.1 / FAT 11.8 / CARBOHYDRATE 30.4 / CHOLESTEROL 28 / IRON 3.0 / SODIUM 224 / CALCIUM 296

BRUNCH TORTILLAS

8 (6-inch) flour tortillas
Vegetable cooking spray
1 teaspoon vegetable oil
½ cup peeled, shredded potato
3 green onions with tops, chopped
1 clove garlic, minced
1 medium tomato, seeded and chopped
1 tablespoon plus 1½ teaspoons chopped green chiles
1 tablespoon chopped green pepper
1 tablespoon chopped sweet red pepper
7 eggs, beaten
2 cups chopped cooked chicken breast (skinned before
  cooking and cooked without salt)
¼ teaspoon salt
⅛ teaspoon pepper
½ cup picante sauce
2 green onions (optional)

Wrap tortillas in aluminum foil; bake at 350° for 10 minutes or until thoroughly heated. Set aside and keep warm.

Coat a large skillet with cooking spray; add oil, and place over medium heat until hot. Add potato, chopped green onions, and garlic; sauté vegetables 3 minutes. Add tomato, green chiles, green pepper, and red pepper; sauté vegetables 2 minutes or until tender. Add eggs, chicken salt, and pepper. Cook, stirring occasionally, until eggs are firm but still moist.

Spoon ½ cup egg mixture onto each warm tortilla. Roll tortillas, and place seam side up on a serving platter. Spoon 1 tablespoon picante sauce over each tortilla. Garnish with green onions, if desired. Serve immediately. Yield: 8 servings (260 calories per serving).

PROTEIN 19.3 / FAT 9.1 / CARBOHYDRATE 26.6 / CHOLESTEROL 269 / IRON 2.4 / SODIUM 270 / CALCIUM 64

GRILLED CRAB TORTILLAS

¾ cup part-skim ricotta cheese
2 tablespoons finely chopped jalapeño pepper
2 tablespoons finely chopped fresh cilantro
2 tablespoons finely chopped green onion
1 tablespoon lime juice
¼ teaspoon salt
½ pound fresh crabmeat, drained and flaked
2 teaspoons margarine, softened
4 (8-inch) whole wheat flour tortillas
Vegetable cooking spray

Combine first 6 ingredients in a small bowl; mix well. Fold in crabmeat, and set aside.

Spread margarine equally on one side of each tortilla; set aside.

Place 1 tortilla, margarine side down, in a nonstick skillet coated with cooking spray. Spread ½ cup crab mixture over half of tortilla in skillet, leaving a ¼-inch margin on sides. Cook over medium heat 3 minutes or until underside of tortilla is golden brown. Fold in half. Transfer to a serving platter, and keep warm. Repeat with remaining ingredients. Serve hot. Yield: 4 servings (198 calories per serving).

PROTEIN 17.6 / FAT 7.3 / CARBOHYDRATE 16.1 / FIBER 1.5 / CHOLESTEROL 71 / SODIUM 522 / POTASSIUM 261

BEAN BURRITOS

Vegetable cooking spray
1 medium onion, chopped
1 clove garlic, minced
2 medium tomatoes, chopped
1 (15-ounce) can pinto beans, drained and rinsed
1 teaspoon ground cumin
½ to 1 teaspoon minced, pickled jalapeño peppers
10 (8-inch) whole wheat flour tortillas
½ medium avocado, peeled and chopped
2 tablespoons minced fresh coriander or 1½ teaspoons
    dried whole cilantro
¾ cup (3 ounces) shredded Monterey Jack cheese

Coat a large saucepan with cooking spray; place over medium heat until hot. Add onion and garlic; sauté until tender. Stir in tomatoes, beans, cumin, and jalapeño peppers; simmer, uncovered, 30 minutes or until mixture is a thick paste, stirring and mashing beans with a wooden spoon. Set aside, and keep warm.

Wrap tortillas in aluminum foil, and bake at 350° for 10 to 15 minutes or until thoroughly heated. Spoon 2 tablespoons bean mixture onto each tortilla; top with remaining ingredients, and roll up. Place on a warm platter, and serve immediately. Yield: 5 servings (266 calories per 2-burrito serving).

PROTEIN 11.7 / FAT 9.3 / CARBOHYDRATE 37.3 / FIBER 3.5 / CHOLESTEROL 12 / SODIUM 229 / POTASSIUM 419

FIESTA BURRITOS

10 (6-inch) flour tortillas
1 pound lean ground pork
1 large onion, chopped
2 cloves garlic, minced
3 tablespoons chopped green chiles
1 teaspoon chili powder, divided
¼ teaspoon ground cumin
¼ teaspoon pepper
3 drops of hot sauce
1¼ cups (5 ounces) shredded 40% less-fat Cheddar
 cheese
1 large tomato, chopped
Vegetable cooking spray
10 cups shredded iceberg lettuce
¾ cup low-fat sour cream
2 drops of hot sauce
Fresh cilantro sprigs (optional)

Wrap tortillas in aluminum foil, and bake at 325° for 15 minutes or until thoroughly heated.

Combine ground pork, onion, and garlic in a large nonstick skillet; cook over medium heat until browned, stirring to crumble. Drain and pat dry with paper towels. Wipe pan drippings from skillet with a paper towel.

Return meat mixture to skillet; stir in green chiles, ½ teaspoon chili powder, cumin, pepper, and 3 drops of hot sauce.

Spoon ⅓ cup meat mixture onto each tortilla; top with 2 tablespoons cheese and tomato. Roll up and secure with wooden picks; place seam side up in an 11-× 7-× 2-inch baking dish that has been coated with cooking spray. Cover and bake at 350° for 20 minutes.

To serve, place each burrito on 1 cup lettuce. Combine sour cream, remaining ½ teaspoon chili powder, and 2 drops of hot sauce. Drizzle sour cream mixture over each burrito. Garnish with fresh cilantro sprigs, if desired. Yield: 10 servings (286 calories per serving).

PROTEIN 17.4 / FAT 12.5 / CARBOHYDRATE 27.7 / CHOLESTEROL 39 / IRON 1.7 / SODIUM 144 / CALCIUM 179

CHEESE ENCHILADAS

1 cup (4 ounces) shredded sharp Cheddar cheese
¼ cup minced, seeded green chiles
½ cup plus 2 tablespoons minced onion, divided
8 (8-inch) corn tortillas
Vegetable cooking spray
¾ cup diced red pepper
1 clove garlic, minced
1 cup chopped tomato
2 drops hot sauce

Combine cheese, green chiles, and 2 tablespoons onion in a bowl. Spoon mixture down centers of tortillas, and roll up. Arrange in an 8-inch square baking dish coated with cooking spray, and set aside.

Coat a skillet with cooking spray; place over medium heat until hot. Add red pepper, ½ cup onion, and garlic; sauté 2 to 3 minutes or until tender. Add tomato and hot sauce; cook 1 minute. Place mixture in container of an electric blender, and process until smooth. Return to skillet, and keep warm.

Cover and bake prepared enchiladas at 400° for 7 minutes or until cheese melts. To serve, top with warm tomato mixture. Yield: 4 servings (358 calories per 2-enchilada serving).

PROTEIN 13.9 / FAT 12.1 / CARBOHYDRATE 51.2 / FIBER 1.6 / CHOLESTEROL 30 / SODIUM 249 / POTASSIUM 258

VEGETABLE-ENCHILADA CASSEROLE

1 small eggplant, peeled and quartered
1 medium zucchini, sliced
½ pound fresh mushrooms, sliced
1 small green pepper, seeded and quartered
Vegetable cooking spray
2 cloves garlic, minced
½ cup chopped green onions
1 (8-ounce) can no-salt-added tomato sauce
1 medium tomato, chopped
1 (4-ounce) can chopped green chiles, drained
1 teaspoon sugar
½ teaspoon chili powder
⅛ teaspoon ground cumin
6 (8-inch) flour tortillas
¾ cup (3 ounces) shredded 40% less-fat Cheddar cheese
¾ cup (3 ounces) shredded Monterey Jack cheese
¼ cup sliced ripe olives
2½ cups shredded lettuce
1 medium tomato, chopped
¼ cup chopped green onions
3 tablespoons low-fat sour cream

Position slicing disc in food processor bowl; top with cover. Arrange eggplant in food chute; slice applying medium pressure with food pusher. Repeat procedure with zucchini, mushrooms, and green pepper. Set aside.

Coat a large nonstick skillet with cooking spray; place over medium-high heat until hot. Add garlic and ½ cup green onions, and sauté until tender. Add reserved vegetables; cover and cook 5 minutes or until tender, stirring occasionally. Stir in tomato sauce and next 5 ingredients; cover and simmer 30 minutes.

Coat at 13- × 9- × 2-inch baking dish with cooking spray. Arrange half of tortillas in dish; top with vegetable mixture. Arrange remaining tortillas over vegetable mixture. Cover and bake at 350° for 20 to 30 minutes or until thoroughly heated. Sprinkle with shredded cheeses and olives. Bake an additional 5 minutes or until cheese melts. To serve, place shredded lettuce on a large serving platter. Spoon casserole over lettuce. Top with chopped tomato, ¼ cup green onions, and 3 tablespoons sour cream. Yield: 6 servings (336 calories per serving).

PROTEIN 14.4 / FAT 12.2 / CARBOHYDRATE 47.6 / CHOLESTEROL 14 / IRON 3.4 / SODIUM 259 / CALCIUM 313

SOUTHWESTERN CHICKEN KIEV

3 tablespoons margarine, softened
3 tablespoons (¾ ounce) shredded Monterey Jack cheese with jalapeño peppers
2 tablespoons minced fresh cilantro
1 teaspoon minced onion
¼ teaspoon garlic powder
Dash of pepper
6 boneless chicken breast halves (1½ pounds), skinned
⅓ cup fine, dry breadcrumbs
½ teaspoon chili powder
¼ cup skim milk
Vegetable cooking spray
3 cups finely shredded iceberg lettuce
1 large tomato, cut into 8 wedges
Fresh cilantro sprigs

Combine first 6 ingredients in a small bowl; stir well. Shape mixture into a 3- × 2-inch stick. Cover and freeze 30 minutes or until firm.

Trim excess fat from chicken. Rinse chicken with cold water, and pat dry. Place chicken between 2 sheets of wax paper; flatten to ¼-inch thickness, using a meat mallet or rolling pan.

Remove margarine stick from freezer, and cut crosswise into 6 portions; place one portion in center of each chicken breast half. Fold long sides of chicken over margarine; fold ends over, and secure with wooden picks.

Combine breadcrumbs and chili powder. Dip each chicken breast half in skim milk, and coat with breadcrumb mixture. Place chicken, seam side up, in a 12-× 8-× 2-inch baking dish coated with cooking spray. Bake at 400° for 15 minutes; turn chicken rolls, and bake an additional 15 minutes or until chicken is tender.

To serve, place shredded lettuce on a serving platter. Top with chicken, and garnish with tomato wedges and cilantro sprigs. Yield: 6 servings (240 calories per serving).

PROTEIN 28.4 / FAT 10.2 / CARBOHYDRATE 7.6 / CHOLESTEROL 74 / IRON 1.5 / SODIUM 202 / CALCIUM 71

CHICKEN PICADILLO TACOS

Vegetable cooking spray
½ pound ground chicken
¼ cup chopped onion
¼ cup chopped sweet red pepper
1 clove garlic, minced
⅓ cup peeled, chopped tomato
2 tablespoons canned low-sodium chicken broth, undiluted
¼ cup peeled, diced apple
1 tablespoon chopped pickled jalapeño pepper
1½ teaspoons cider vinegar
¼ teaspoon ground cumin
¼ teaspoon ground cinnamon
⅛ teaspoon salt
2 tablespoons raisins
4 taco shells
1 cup shredded iceberg lettuce
½ cup (2 ounces) shredded Monterey Jack cheese

Coat a large nonstick skillet with cooking spray. Place over medium heat until hot. Add chicken, onion, red pepper, and garlic; cook until chicken is browned, stirring frequently. Add tomato and next 7 ingredients. Bring to a boil; reduce heat, and simmer 8 minutes or until thickened. Stir in raisins.

Heat taco shells according to package directions. Spoon ½ cup chicken mixture into each shell. Top each taco with ¼ cup shredded lettuce and 2 tablespoons cheese. Serve immediately. Yield: 4 servings (203 calories per serving).

PROTEIN 18.2 / FAT 8.2 / CARBOHYDRATE 13.8 / CHOLESTEROL 44 / IRON 1.5 / SODIUM 310 / CALCIUM 129

MEXICAN-STYLE CHICKEN ROLL-UPS

8 boneless chicken breast halves (2 pounds), skinned
4 canned whole green chiles, halved and seeded
3 ounces Monterey Jack cheese, cut into 8 strips
¾ cup fine, dry breadcrumbs
1 tablespoon chili powder
1½ teaspoons ground cumin
¼ teaspoon salt
¼ teaspoon garlic powder
¼ cup skim milk
Vegetable cooking spray
4 cups shredded lettuce
½ cup commercial picante sauce
¼ cup plain low-fat yogurt

Trim excess fat from chicken. Place each chicken breast half between 2 sheets of waxed paper; flatten to ¼-inch thickness, using a meat mallet or rolling pin.

Place a green chile half and one strip of cheese in center of each chicken breast half; roll up lengthwise, tucking edges under. Secure with wooden picks.

Combine breadcrumbs, chili powder, cumin, salt, and garlic powder. Dip chicken rolls in milk; dredge in breadcrumb mixture, coating well. Place chicken in a 12- × 8- × 2-inch baking dish coated with cooking spray. Bake at 400° for 30 minutes or until chicken is done.

Place each chicken roll on ½ cup shredded lettuce; top each

with 1 tablespoon picante sauce and 1½ teaspoons yogurt. Serve immediately. Yield: 8 servings (236 calories per serving).

PROTEIN 30.7 / FAT 7.1 / CARBOHYDRATE 10.6 / FIBER 0.7 / CHOLESTEROL 80 / SODIUM 405 / POTASSIUM 392

GRILLED ROUND STEAK WITH TOMATILLO SAUCE

1½ pounds beef top round steak (about ¾-inch thick)
¾ cup Burgundy or other dry red wine
2 tablespoons lime juice
1 tablespoon Worcestershire sauce
½ teaspoon seasoned salt
Dash of pepper
1 clove garlic, minced
Vegetable cooking spray
Tomatillo Sauce

Trim excess fat from steak. Place steak in a large shallow baking dish. Combine next 6 ingredients in a small bowl; mix well, and pour over steak. Cover and refrigerate 24 hours, turning steak occasionally.

Remove steak from marinade. Coat grill with cooking spray. Grill 5 to 6 inches over hot coals 5 to 7 minutes on each side or until desired degree of doneness. Transfer steak to a cutting board; cut steak across grain into ¼-inch-thick slices. Serve immediately with equal amounts of Tomatillo Sauce per serving. Yield: 6 servings (215 calories per serving).

Tomatillo Sauce:

½ pound fresh tomatillos
1 small onion, chopped
1 clove garlic, peeled
½ cup loosely packed cilantro leaves

1 tablespoon vegetable oil
½ teaspoon sugar
½ teaspoon salt

Remove stems and outer husks of tomatillos; rinse well. Combine all ingredients in container of an electric blender; process until smooth. Transfer tomatillo mixture to a medium saucepan, and bring to a boil. Reduce heat, and simmer, uncovered, 10 minutes. Serve hot. Yield: about 1 cup.

PROTEIN 27.7 / FAT 6.9 / CARBOHYDRATE 4.4 / FIBER 0.5 / CHOLESTEROL 55 / SODIUM 441 / POTASSIUM 504

BEEF WITH TOMATILLOS

1½ pounds lean round steak
Vegetable cooking spray
1⅓ cups chopped onion
2 cloves garlic, minced
1 cup husked and chopped tomatillos
½ cup water
1 tablespoon chopped jalapeño peppers
1 teaspoon dried coriander
½ teaspoon dried whole marjoram
¼ teaspoon salt
⅛ teaspoon crushed red pepper
½ cup low-fat sour cream
2 tablespoons minced fresh cilantro

Trim fat from steak; cut into 1-inch pieces. Coat a large nonstick skillet with cooking spray. Place over medium-high heat until hot. Add steak; cook until browned, stirring often. Remove steak; drain and pat dry with paper towels. Wipe pan drippings from skillet with a paper towel.

Coat skillet with cooking spray. Place over medium-high heat until hot. Add onion and garlic; sauté 5 minutes or until tender. Return steak to skillet; add tomatillos and next 6 ingredients, stirring well. Bring mixture to a boil; cover, reduce heat, and simmer 1 hour or until meat is tender. Place beef on 6 individual serving plates. Top each serving evenly with sour cream and fresh cilantro. Yield: 6 servings (216 calories per serving).

PROTEIN 26.0 / FAT 9.6 / CARBOHYDRATE 5.4 / CHOLESTEROL 78 / IRON 2.8 / SODIUM 166 / CALCIUM 42

TEXAS STEAK WITH GRAVY

1½ pounds lean round steak
½ teaspoon pepper
¼ teaspoon salt
Vegetable cooking spray
1 teaspoon vegetable oil
⅓ cup evaporated skimmed milk
⅓ cup water
1 tablespoon all-purpose flour
2 tablespoons strong brewed coffee
¼ teaspoon pepper
⅛ teaspoon salt

Trim fat from steak. Place steak between 2 sheets of wax paper; flatten to ½-inch thickness. Cut steak into 6 equal pieces. Combine ½ teaspoon pepper and ¼ teaspoon salt, stirring well. Sprinkle evenly over steak pieces.

Coat a large nonstick skillet with cooking spray; add oil. Place over medium-high heat until hot. Add steak, and cook 3 minutes on each side or until browned. Remove steak; drain and pat dry with paper towels. Place steak on a serving platter, and keep warm. Wipe pan drippings from skillet with a paper towel.

Combine milk, water, and flour; stir until smooth. Add to skillet. Cook over low heat until thickened, stirring constantly. Stir in remaining ingredients. Cook over low heat until thoroughly heated. Pour over steak, and serve. Yield: 6 servings (192 calories per serving).

PROTEIN 25.8 / FAT 7.8 / CARBOHYDRATE 2.9 / CHOLESTEROL 71 / IRON 2.5 / SODIUM 218 / CALCIUM 48

MEXICAN BEEF STEW WITH TORTILLA DUMPLINGS

1 pound ground chuck
½ teaspoon beef-flavored bouillon granules
1 teaspoon ground cumin
1 teaspoon minced fresh cilantro
½ teaspoon pepper
½ teaspoon dried whole oregano
½ teaspoon dried whole basil
2 (4-ounce) cans chopped green chiles, drained
2½ cups water
2½ cups spicy hot vegetable juice cocktail
3 (6-inch) flour tortillas, cut into 1-inch pieces

Cook ground chuck in a large Dutch oven over medium heat until browned, stirring to crumble. Drain and pat dry with paper towels. Wipe pan drippings from Dutch oven with a paper towel.

Return meat to Dutch oven; add remaining ingredients except tortillas. Bring to a boil; cover, reduce heat, and simmer 1 hour. Add tortillas; cover and cook an additional 20 minutes or until tortillas have expanded to resemble dumplings. Yield: 6 cups (240 calories per 1-cup serving).

PROTEIN 15.5 / FAT 11.7 / CARBOHYDRATE 17.2 / CHOLESTEROL 44 / IRON 2.3 / SODIUM 370 / CALCIUM 26

FAJITAS

2 pounds flank steak
¼ cup lemon juice
¼ cup lime juice
1 (2½-inch) green chile, seeded and minced
1 tablespoon vegetable oil
¼ teaspoon salt
¼ teaspoon pepper
¼ teaspoon ground cumin
8 (6-inch) flour tortillas

Trim excess fat from steak; place in a shallow baking dish, and set aside.

Combine lemon juice, lime juice, green chile, oil, salt, pepper, and cumin, stirring well; pour over steak. Cover and marinate in refrigerator 4 hours or overnight.

Drain steak, reserving marinade. Place on rack in a broiler pan. Broil 5 to 6 inches from heat 5 to 6 minutes on each side or until desired degree of doneness, basting often with reserved marinade. Transfer to a cutting board; slice steak diagonally across the grain into thin slices.

Place a skillet or griddle over medium heat until hot. Place tortillas in skillet 30 to 40 seconds on each side or until thoroughly heated. Divide steak slices evenly among tortillas. Wrap tortilla around steak; serve with Fresh Tomato Salsa (see page 70), if desired. Yield: 8 servings (296 calories per serving).

PROTEIN 29.9 / FAT 8.0 / CARBOHYDRATE 26.2 / FIBER 0.5 / CHOLESTEROL 55 / SODIUM 132 / POTASSIUM 494

NEW MEXICO GREEN CHILE STEW

¾ pound poblano chiles
1 pound boneless pork
Vegetable cooking spray
1 medium onion, chopped
1 cup peeled, cubed red potato
2 cloves garlic, minced
2 cups water
2 teaspoons chicken-flavored bouillon granules
¼ teaspoon salt
¼ cup finely chopped cilantro
1½ cups water
1 tablespoon cornstarch
Fresh cilantro sprigs (optional)

Wash and dry peppers; place on a baking sheet. Broil 3 to 4 inches from heat, turning often with tongs, until blistered on all sides. Immediately place peppers in a plastic bag; seal and let stand 10 minutes to loosen skins. Peel peppers; remove core and seeds. Chop peppers.

Trim fat from pork; cut meat into 1-inch pieces. Coat a large Dutch oven with cooking spray, place over medium-high heat until hot. Add pork and onion; cook, stirring frequently, until meat is browned on all sides. Add potatoes, garlic, 2 cups water, bouillon granules, and salt. Bring to a boil, cover, reduce heat, and simmer 45 minutes. Add reserved peppers and cilantro; simmer an additional 15 minutes.

Combine 1½ cups water and cornstarch, stirring until blended. Gradually add cornstarch mixture to meat mixture; cook over medium heat until thickened. To serve, ladle stew into individual serving bowls. Garnish with fresh cilantro sprigs, if desired. Yield: 6 cups (185 calories per 1-cup serving).

PROTEIN 18.9 / FAT 6.0 / CARBOHYDRATE 14.0 / CHOLESTEROL 48 / IRON 1.8 / SODIUM 428 / CALCIUM 31

CRAB-PAPAYA VERACRUZ

3 ripe papayas
Curly leaf lettuce leaves
Vegetable cooking spray
1 teaspoon unsalted margarine
¼ cup chopped green onions
¼ cup chopped green pepper
¼ cup chopped sweet red pepper
2 medium tomatoes, seeded and chopped
¼ cup tomato and green chile cocktail
1 tablespoon lime juice
1 tablespoon chopped fresh cilantro
½ teaspoon dried whole oregano
¾ pound fresh lump crabmeat, drained and flaked
Fresh cilantro sprigs (optional)

Cut papayas in half lengthwise; scoop out and discard seeds. (Cut a thin slice from bottom of each papaya half, allowing it to sit flat, if necessary.) Place papaya halves, cut side up, on a lettuce-lined platter; set aside.

Coat a large nonstick skillet with cooking spray; add margarine. Place over medium heat until hot. Add green onions, green pepper, and red pepper; sauté until tender. Add tomato and next 4 ingredients; cook 2 minutes, stirring occasionally. Add crabmeat, stirring well; cook 2 minutes or until thoroughly heated. Mound ½ cup crab mixture into each papaya half using a slotted spoon. If desired, garnish each serving with fresh cilantro sprigs. Yield: 6 servings (149 calories per serving).

PROTEIN 13.0 / FAT 2.1 / CARBOHYDRATE 21.3 / CHOLESTEROL 30 / IRON 1.2 / SODIUM 620 / CALCIUM 88

SWORDFISH VERACRUZ

4 swordfish steaks (1 pound)
¼ teaspoon pepper
Vegetable cooking spray
2 teaspoons margarine
½ cup chopped onion
1 clove garlic, crushed
1 medium tomato, chopped
2 tablespoons chopped green chiles
1 tablespoon Chablis or other dry white wine
1 tablespoon white wine vinegar
¼ teaspoon salt

Rinse swordfish with cold water, and pat dry. Sprinkle with pepper. Coat a skillet with cooking spray; add margarine, and place over medium heat until margarine melts. Add fish to skillet, and cook until browned on both sides; place in a 10- × 6- × 2-inch baking dish.

Wipe skillet with a paper towel, and coat with cooking spray. Place over medium heat until hot. Add onion and garlic, and sauté until tender. Add tomato, green chiles, wine, vinegar, and salt; bring to a boil. Remove from heat, and spoon mixture over steaks. Bake, uncovered, at 450° for 10 minutes or until steaks flake easily when tested with a fork. Remove steaks from dish to a warm platter, using a slotted spoon. Yield: 4 servings (169 calories per serving).

PROTEIN 22.4 / FAT 6.6 / CARBOHYDRATE 3.9 / FIBER 0.5 / CHOLESTEROL 62 / SODIUM 243 / POTASSIUM 637

Create a new family favorite with Tortilla Torte (page 34) surrounded by lettuce. This meatless dish has hearty flavor that's sure to please everyone.

This fiesta includes Fajitas (page 49) (front), Seviche, and Guacamole Salad (page 25).

Tomato Salsa (page 70) will appeal to those who like their relish with a zip of Latin American flavor.

The mild flavor of tofu is enhanced by the spicy, Mexican flavors of jalapeno pepper, tomato, avocado, and cilantro in Tofu Chalupas (page 54)—just one of the many ways to incorporate tofu (a protein-, iron-, and calcium-rich food) into your meal plans.

The spicy, hot Southwestern flavors of jalapeno peppers and cilantro are tempered with the mild flavor of chicken, crisp shredded lettuce, and fresh tomato slices in this palate-pleasing Southwestern Chicken Kiev (page 42).

Fresh cilantro adds south-of-the-border taste to Ensalada Tostada (page 27), a satisfying Mexican salad.

Southern-style Spicy Red Beans and Chunky Rice (page 56) makes a hearty, satisfying vegetarian meal.

Crab-Papaya Veracruz (page 51) makes a refreshing main course for a leisurely brunch.

Fresh cilantro and three colors of sweet pepper rings add a lively spark to a spicy Mexican Pizza (page 55).

Ground cumin and red pepper give Mexican Black Beans 'n' Rice (page 65) authentic south-of-the-border flavor.

Savour the flavors of the Southwest with Beefy-Tortilla Pie (page 33) and Southwestern Jicama Salad (page 26).

The best dessert is one that's guilt-free; experience the pleasure without penitence when you serve a fruit-based dish such as Rum Compote in Tortilla Shells (page 76).

SPICY BEAN CHALUPAS

1½ cups dried pinto beans
4 cups water
1 (4-ounce) can chopped green chiles, undrained
⅓ cup chopped green onions
1½ teaspoons ground cumin
½ teaspoon salt
½ teaspoon dried whole oregano
½ teaspoon dried Italian seasoning
6 (6-inch) corn tortillas
3 cups shredded lettuce
1 small tomato, chopped
1 cup (4 ounces) shredded Monterey Jack cheese with
   jalapeño peppers
¼ cup plus 2 tablespoons plain low-fat yogurt
2 tablespoons sliced ripe olives

Sort and wash pinto beans; place in a large Dutch oven. Add water to cover, and let beans soak overnight.

Drain beans; return to Dutch oven and add 4 cups water. Add green chiles and next 5 ingredients, stirring well. Bring to a boil; cover, reduce heat, and simmer 1½ hours. Pour 1 cup of bean mixture into container of an electric blender or food processor; process until smooth. Return pureed bean mixture to Dutch oven. Cover and simmer 30 minutes. Uncover and simmer an additional 15 to 20 minutes or until mixture is thickened and liquid is absorbed; stir frequently.

Wrap tortillas in aluminum foil. Bake at 350° for 10 minutes or until thoroughly heated. Unwrap, and spread ½ cup bean mixture over each tortilla. To serve, place each tortilla on ½ cup shredded lettuce. Sprinkle chopped tomato and cheese evenly over top of tortillas. Top each serving with 1 tablespoon yogurt and 1 teaspoon sliced olives. Serve immediately. Yield: 6 servings (299 calories per serving).

PROTEIN 17.4 / FAT 7.7 / CARBOHYDRATE 42.1 / CHOLESTEROL 16 / IRON 4.8 / SODIUM 371 / CALCIUM 274

TOFU CHALUPAS

Vegetable cooking spray
⅓ cup finely chopped onion
1 (10½-ounce) package tofu, drained and crumbled
2 cloves garlic, crushed
2 tomatoes, seeded and chopped
1 jalapeño pepper, seeded and chopped
¼ teaspoon chili powder
¼ teaspoon ground cumin
½ teaspoon dried whole oregano
2 tablespoons chopped fresh cilantro
4 (6-inch) corn tortillas
½ cup shredded iceberg lettuce
½ medium avocado, peeled and chopped
¼ cup (1 ounce) shredded Cheddar cheese

Coat a large skillet with cooking spray; place over medium heat until hot. Add onion, and sauté until tender. Add tofu and garlic, and cook for 3 minutes, stirring constantly. Stir in tomatoes, jalapeño pepper, chili powder, cumin, oregano, and cilantro, and continue to cook over medium heat, stirring frequently, until thoroughly heated.

Wrap tortillas in aluminum foil, and bake at 350° for 10 minutes or until thoroughly heated. Top each tortilla with one-fourth of lettuce, tofu mixture, avocado, and cheese. Serve immediately. Yield: 4 servings (216 calories per serving).

PROTEIN 11.7 / FAT 9.9 / CARBOHYDRATE 23.9 / CHOLESTEROL 7 / IRON 4.3 / SODIUM 120 / CALCIUM 221

MEXICAN PIZZA

¾ cup warm water (105° to 115°), divided
1 package dry yeast
1 teaspoon sugar
1½ cups all-purpose flour
½ cup yellow cornmeal
¼ teaspoon garlic powder
¼ teaspoon freshly ground pepper
Vegetable cooking spray
¾ pound lean ground beef
¼ cup chopped onion
1 jalapeño pepper, seeded and minced
½ teaspoon salt
¼ teaspoon ground cumin
1 cup no-salt-added tomato sauce
¾ cup seeded, chopped tomato
3 tablespoons minced fresh cilantro
1 medium-size sweet red, yellow, or green pepper,
 sliced into rings
3 tablespoons sliced ripe olives
1 cup (4 ounces) shredded Monterey Jack cheese

Combine ¼ cup water, yeast, and sugar in a small bowl; let stand 5 minutes.

Position knife blade in food processor bowl. Add flour, cornmeal, garlic powder, and freshly ground pepper; top with cover, and process 10 seconds. Add yeast mixture, and process until blended. With processor running, slowly add enough of remaining ½ cup water to form a ball that leaves sides of bowl; continue processing 15 to 20 seconds after dough forms a ball. Let stand 2 minutes. With processor running, add enough remaining water to make a soft, smooth dough; process 10 to 15 seconds.

Turn dough out onto a 15-inch pizza pan that has been coated with cooking spray. Shape dough into a ball; cover and let stand 10 minutes. Pat dough evenly into pan. Bake at 425° for 5 minutes; set aside.

Coat a large nonstick skillet with cooking spray; place over medium heat until hot. Add ground beef and next 4 ingredients; cook until meat is browned, stirring to crumble meat. Drain and pat dry with paper towels; set aside.

Combine tomato sauce, chopped tomato, and cilantro. Spread mixture over crust, leaving a ½-inch border around edges. Top with ground beef mixture, pepper rings, and olives. Sprinkle cheese evenly over pizza. Bake at 425° for 15 to 20 minutes or until crust is lightly browned and cheese melts. Yield: 6 servings (388 calories per serving).

PROTEIN 20.7 / FAT 15.0 / CARBOHYDRATE 41.6 / CHOLESTEROL 48 / IRON 3.3 / SODIUM 396 / CALCIUM 167

SPICY RED BEANS AND CHUNKY RICE

¾ pound dried red kidney beans
2 cups water
Vegetable cooking spray
1 tablespoon plus 1½ teaspoons vegetable oil
1¼ cups chopped onion
2 cloves garlic, minced
2½ cups water
2 bay leaves
1 tablespoon beef-flavored bouillon granules
½ teaspoon dried whole oregano
½ teaspoon hot sauce
1 tablespoon honey
Chunky Rice
Fresh oregano sprigs (optional)

Sort and wash beans. Place beans and 2 cups water in a medium saucepan; bring to a boil. Cover, remove from heat, and let stand 1 hour. Drain beans and set aside.

Coat a large Dutch oven with cooking spray; add oil. Place over medium-high heat until hot. Add onion and garlic, and sauté until tender. Add beans, 2½ cups water, and next 5 ingredients; bring to a boil. Cover, reduce heat, and simmer 2 hours, or until beans are tender. Remove and discard bay leaves. Serve over Chunky Rice. Garnish with oregano sprigs, if desired. Yield: 8 servings (323 calories per serving).

Chunky Rice:

Vegetable cooking spray
1 cup chopped onion
1 cup finely chopped carrot
1 cup finely chopped celery
¾ cup finely chopped sweet red pepper
½ cup finely chopped green pepper
2 cloves garlic, minced
1⅓ cups uncooked long-grain rice
1 teaspoon cajun seasoning
2 tablespoons chopped fresh parsley

Coat a large nonstick skillet with cooking spray; place over medium-high heat until hot. Add onion and next 5 ingredients, and sauté until tender. Set aside.

Cook rice according to package directions, omitting salt and fat and adding 1 teaspoon cajun seasoning.

Toss vegetable mixture, rice, and parsley. Yield: 4 cups.

PROTEIN 13.2 / FAT 3.9 / CARBOHYDRATE 59.8 / CHOLESTEROL 0 / IRON 5.1 / SODIUM 417 / CALCIUM 98

MEXICAN STUFFED PEPPERS

6 medium-size green peppers
1 cup cooked long-grain rice (cooked without salt or fat)
1 cup cooked lentils
¾ cup spicy hot vegetable juice cocktail
½ cup frozen whole kernel corn, thawed
2 tablespoons diced pimiento

½ teaspoon ground cumin
1 cup (4 ounces) shredded reduced-fat Monterey Jack
cheese with jalapeño peppers, divided

Cut tops off peppers, and remove seeds. Cook peppers in boiling water 5 minutes. Drain and set peppers aside.

Combine rice and next 5 ingredients in a medium bowl: stir well. Stir in ½ cup cheese.

Spoon rice mixture evenly into peppers; place peppers in an 11- × 7- × 2-inch baking dish. Add hot water to pan to a depth of ½ inch. Cover and bake at 350° for 25 minutes. Sprinkle remaining ½ cup cheese over peppers; bake, uncovered, an additional 5 minutes or until cheese melts. Serve warm. Yield: 6 servings (191 calories per serving).

PROTEIN 10.9 / FAT 4.8 / CARBOHYDRATE 28.5 / CHOLESTEROL 13 / IRON 3.3 / SODIUM 218 / CALCIUM 19

STUFFED ONIONS IN GUACAMOLE SAUCE

4 medium onions
½ pound ground chuck
¼ cup chopped green pepper
½ teaspoon pepper
¼ teaspoon salt
¼ teaspoon chili powder
¼ teaspoon ground cumin
1 small avocado, coarsely chopped
½ cup (2 ounces) shredded Monterey Jack cheese
¼ cup plus 2 tablespoons skim milk
2 tablespoons low-fat sour cream
1 tablespoon lemon juice
1 teaspoon minced fresh cilantro
⅛ teaspoon garlic powder
⅛ teaspoon Worcestershire sauce

Peel onions; cut a thin slice from top of each. Place onions in a vegetable steamer over boiling water. Cover and steam 5 minutes or until tender. Let cool. Scoop out centers, leaving ¼-inch-thick shells. Set aside.

Combine ground chuck and next 5 ingredients; stir well. Cook ground chuck mixture in a large nonstick skillet over medium heat until browned, stirring to crumble. Drain and pat dry with paper towels. Spoon mixture evenly into reserved onion shells; place in a shallow baking dish. Bake at 350° for 10 minutes.

Combine avocado and remaining ingredients in container of an electric blender; process until smooth. Place onions on 4 individual serving plates. Spoon ¼ cup sauce around each onion. Serve immediately. Yield: 4 servings (290 calories per serving).

PROTEIN 17.1 / FAT 18.4 / CARBOHYDRATE 15.5 / CHOLESTEROL 48 / IRON 2.2 / SODIUM 271 / CALCIUM 190

SIDE DISHES

MEXICAN CORN PUDDING

Vegetable cooking spray
1 medium onion, chopped
1 medium-size green pepper, seeded and chopped
1 (17-ounce) can whole kernel corn, drained
1 (10-ounce) can chopped tomatoes with green chiles,
   drained
¼ cup all-purpose flour
¼ teaspoon pepper
2 cups skim milk
1 egg, beaten
¼ cup (1 ounce) shredded extra-sharp Cheddar cheese

Coat a large skillet with cooking spray, and place over medium heat until hot. Add onion and green pepper. Sauté until tender. Remove from heat.

Position knife in food processor bowl; add corn, and pulse 10 to 12 times or until corn is coarsely chopped. Add corn and tomatoes with green chiles to mixture in skillet; add flour and pepper, stirring well. Gradually add milk, egg, and cheese, stirring until well blended.

Coat 8 (6-ounce) custard cups with cooking spray. Divide corn mixture evenly among them. Place 4 custard cups in a 9-inch square baking pan; fill pan with boiling water to a depth of 1 inch. Repeat with remaining custard cups.

Bake at 325° for 1 hour and 15 minutes or until knife inserted in center comes out clean. Remove cups from water; let stand 5 minutes. Serve hot. Yield: 8 servings (124 calories per serving).

PROTEIN 6.1 / FAT 2.7 / CARBOHYDRATE 20.7 / FIBER 0.9 / CHOLESTEROL 39 / SODIUM 121 / POTASSIUM 322

MEXICAN CHEESE GRITS

2¼ cups water
¼ teaspoon salt
¾ cup quick-cooking grits, uncooked
½ cup (2 ounces) shredded sharp Cheddar cheese
1 (4-ounce) can chopped green chiles, drained
1 (2-ounce) jar diced pimiento, drained
1 clove garlic, crushed
¼ teaspoon hot sauce
1 egg, beaten
Vegetable cooking spray

Combine water and salt in a medium saucepan; bring to a boil. Stir in grits. Cover; reduce heat to low, and cook 5 minutes, stirring occasionally. Remove from heat, and add cheese, stirring until cheese melts; stir in green chiles, pimiento, garlic, and hot sauce. Gradually stir one-fourth of hot grits mixture into egg; stir egg mixture into remaining grits mixture. Spoon into a 1-quart baking dish coated with cooking spray. Bake at 350° for 30 minutes or until set. Yield: 6 servings (125 calories per serving).

PROTEIN 5.1 / FAT 4.2 / CARBOHYDRATE 16.3 / FIBER 0.3 / CHOLESTEROL 56 / SODIUM 191 / POTASSIUM 83

MEXICAN HOMINY

Vegetable cooking spray
2 cups chopped, peeled tomato
1 cup chopped onion
1 (15-ounce) can hominy, drained
½ teaspoon chili powder
⅛ teaspoon garlic powder
⅛ teaspoon salt
⅛ teaspoon pepper
¼ cup (1 ounce) shredded Monterey Jack cheese

Coat a medium skillet with cooking spray; place over medium heat until hot. Add tomato and onion, and sauté 5 minutes or until onion is tender; remove from heat. Add hominy, chili powder, garlic powder, salt, and pepper; stir well. Spoon mixture into a 1-quart baking dish coated with cooking spray. Bake, uncovered, at 350° for 25 minutes; sprinkle with cheese, and bake an additional 5 minutes or until cheese melts. Yield: 6 servings (66 calories per serving).

PROTEIN 2.9 / FAT 1.8 / CARBOHYDRATE 11.2 / FIBER 1.2 / CHOLESTEROL 4 / SODIUM 204 / POTASSIUM 210

SEASONED RICE

Vegetable cooking spray
½ cup chopped onion
½ cup chopped sweet red pepper
2½ cups water
1 teaspoon chicken-flavored bouillon granules
½ teaspoon ground cumin
⅛ teaspoon hot sauce
1 cup parboiled rice, uncooked

Coat a medium saucepan with cooking spray; place over medium heat until hot. Add onion and red pepper; sauté 5 minutes or until tender.

Add water, bouillon granules, cumin, and hot sauce; bring to a boil, and stir in rice. Cover; reduce heat, and simmer 20 minutes or until rice is tender and liquid is absorbed. Yield: 8 servings (90 calories per serving).

PROTEIN 1.9 / FAT 0.3 / CARBOHYDRATE 20.2 / FIBER 0.3 / CHOLESTEROL 0 / SODIUM 51 / POTASSIUM 78

JALAPEÑO RICE CASSEROLE

2⅔ cups water
½ teaspoon chicken-flavored bouillon granules
1 cup parboiled rice, uncooked
½ cup plain low-fat yogurt
2 tablespoons reduced-calorie creamy Italian salad dressing
1 jalapeño pepper, seeded and chopped
1 tablespoon chopped fresh parsley
Vegetable cooking spray
⅓ cup (1⅓ ounces) shredded Monterey Jack cheese

Combine water and bouillon granules in a medium saucepan; bring to a boil. Stir in rice. Cover; reduce heat, and simmer 25 minutes or until liquid is absorbed. Remove from heat; stir in yogurt, salad dressing, jalapeño pepper, and parsley.

Spoon into a 1-quart baking dish coated with cooking spray. Bake, uncovered, at 350° for 20 minutes. Top with cheese; bake 5 minutes. Yield: 6 servings (150 calories per serving).

PROTEIN 4.8 / FAT 2.5 / CARBOHYDRATE 27.3 / FIBER 0.1 / CHOLESTEROL 6 / SODIUM 204 / POTASSIUM 114

MEXICAN BLACK BEANS 'N' RICE

2 teaspoons olive oil
1 cup chopped onion
½ cup chopped green pepper
2 cups cooked long-grain rice (cooked without salt or
    fat)
½ teaspoon ground cumin
¼ teaspoon ground red pepper
⅛ teaspoon dried coriander
1 (15-ounce) can black beans, rinsed and drained
¾ cup chopped tomato

Heat olive oil in a large nonstick skillet over medium-high heat until hot. Add onion and green pepper; sauté until tender. Stir in rice and next 3 ingredients; sauté 3 minutes. Add beans and chopped tomato; sauté 3 minutes or until thoroughly heated. Yield: 8 servings (123 calories per ½-cup serving).

PROTEIN 3.8 / FAT 1.5 / CARBOHYDRATE 23.7 / CHOLESTEROL 0 / IRON 1.4 / SODIUM 3 / CALCIUM 19

MEXICAN SPAGHETTI SQUASH

2 (3-pound) spaghetti squash
Vegetable cooking spray
1 small onion, chopped
1 clove garlic, minced
1 (14½-ounce) can no-salt-added whole tomatoes,
    undrained and chopped
1 (4-ounce) can chopped green chiles, drained
½ teaspoon chili powder
⅛ teaspoon red pepper
½ cup (2 ounces) shredded Monterey Jack cheese

Wash squash; pierce with a fork several times. Place squash in a large baking dish. Bake at 350° for 1 hour or until squash yield to pressure. Let cool to touch. Cut squash in half lengthwise; discard seeds. Remove spaghetti-like strands from squash using a fork. Place squash in a large serving bowl. Set aside and keep warm. Discard squash shells.

Coat a large skillet with cooking spray; place over medium-high heat until hot. Add onion and garlic; sauté until tender. Stir in tomatoes, green chiles, chili powder, and red pepper. Bring to a boil. Cover; reduce heat, and simmer 10 minutes. Add tomato mixture and cheese to reserved squash, tossing gently. Serve immediately. Yield: 12 servings (96 calories per serving).

PROTEIN 3.1 / FAT 2.1 / CARBOHYDRATE 17.5 / CHOLESTEROL 4 / IRON 1.1 / SODIUM 185 / CALCIUM 101

CONDIMENTS

FRESH SALSA RELISH

2 tablespoons red wine vinegar
2 tablespoons lime juice
2 teaspoons olive oil
1 medium-size sweet red pepper
1¾ cups peeled, seeded, and chopped tomato
¾ cup minced shallots
1 jalapeño pepper, seeded and minced
2 tablespoons minced fresh cilantro
1 clove garlic, minced
¼ teaspoon salt
¼ teaspoon freshly ground pepper

Combine vinegar, lime juice, and olive oil in a small bowl. Beat well with a wire whisk; set mixture aside.

Cut red pepper in half lengthwise; remove and discard seeds and membrane. Place pepper, skin side up on a baking sheet; flatten with palm of hand. Broil 5½ inches from heat 15 to 20 minutes or until charred. Place in ice water, and chill 5 minutes. Remove pepper from water; peel and discard skin. Dice pepper, and place in a medium bowl.

Add tomato and remaining ingredients to pepper; toss well. Pour reserved vinegar mixture over tomato mixture; toss to combine. Serve with beef, pork, chicken, or unsalted tortilla chips. Yield: 3 cups (6 calories per tablespoon).

PROTEIN 0.2 / FAT 0.2 / CARBOHYDRATE 0.9 / CHOLESTEROL 0 / IRON 0.1 / SODIUM 13 / CALCIUM 2

CREAMY TOMATILLO SAUCE

½ pound fresh tomatillos
¼ cup chopped onion
¼ cup water
1 clove garlic, crushed
¼ teaspoon chicken-flavored bouillon granules
2 tablespoons canned chopped green chiles, drained
2 tablespoons low-fat sour cream

Remove and discard husks from tomatillos; cut tomatillos into quarters, and place in a small saucepan. Add onion and next 3 ingredients. Bring to a boil. Cover, reduce heat, and simmer 7 minutes or until tomatillos are tender.

Pour tomatillo mixture into container of an electric blender or food processor; process until smooth. Press puree through a sieve to remove seeds. Stir in green chiles and sour cream. Serve warm with steaks, hamburgers, or grilled chicken. Yield: 1 cup (7 calories per tablespoon).

PROTEIN 0.3 / FAT 0.3 / CARBOHYDRATE 1.1 / CHOLESTEROL 1 / IRON 0.1 / SODIUM 14 / CALCIUM 4

ANCHO CHILE MAYONNAISE

½ cup reduced-calorie mayonnaise
½ cup soft tofu
1 tablespoon plus 1½ teaspoons Ancho Chile Paste
1 clove garlic, minced
2 teaspoons lime juice
¼ teaspoon salt

Combine all ingredients in container of an electric blender or food processor; process until smooth. Serve with Mexican or chicken salads. Yield: 1 cup (27 calories per tablespoon).

Ancho Chile Paste:

3 dried ancho chiles
6 cups water
2 tablespoons lime juice
1 tablespoon olive oil

Wash chiles, and place in a large saucepan; add 6 cups water. Place a bowl or plate over chiles to keep them submerged. Cover and bring to a boil. Remove from heat, and let chiles stand, covered, 2 hours or until chiles are softened. Drain chiles. Remove and discard stems and seeds.

Place chiles in container of an electric blender or food processor; process until smooth, scraping sides of container occasionally with a spatula. Add lime juice and olive oil; process until mixture is combined. Store in refrigerator or freezer. Use Ancho Chile Paste as a flavoring in Southwestern dishes, stews, or chili. Yield: 1 cup.

PROTEIN 0.6 / FAT 2.4 / CARBOHYDRATE 1.1 / CHOLESTEROL 3 / IRON 0.1 / SODIUM 94 / CALCIUM 14

HOT MEXICAN RELISH

6 green onions, coarsely chopped
2 medium tomatoes, quartered
1 small green pepper, seeded and quartered
1 clove garlic
Vegetable cooking spray
1 (8¾-ounce) can no-salt-added whole kernel corn, drained
1 (4-ounce) can chopped green chiles, drained
3 tablespoons hot chili sauce
1 tablespoon chili powder
1 teaspoon pepper

Position knife blade in food processor bowl; add first 4 ingredients. Top with cover, and process until finely chopped. Coat a large nonstick skillet with cooking spray; place over medium-high heat until hot. Add chopped vegetables, and sauté until tender. Stir in corn and remaining ingredients. Cook over medium heat until thoroughly heated. Serve hot or cold. Yield: 3 cups (7 calories per tablespoon).

PROTEIN 0.2 / FAT 0.1 / CARBOHYDRATE 1.4 / CHOLESTEROL 0 / IRON 0.2 / SODIUM 19 / CALCIUM 3

FRESH TOMATO SALSA

2 cups peeled, seeded, and coarsely chopped tomato
½ cup minced green onion
½ cup tomato sauce
2 tablespoons chopped fresh parsley
2 to 3 teaspoons minced green chile
2 teaspoons lemon juice
¼ teaspoon salt
⅛ teaspoon pepper

Combine all ingredients in a small bowl, stirring gently. Cover and chill at least 4 hours. Serve with Fajitas, if desired. Yield: 2¼ cups (16 calories per ¼-cup serving).

PROTEIN 0.7 / FAT 0.1 / CARBOHYDRATE 3.4 / FIBER 0.5 / CHOLESTEROL 0 / SODIUM 125 / POTASSIUM 164

TOMATO SALSA

3 medium tomatoes, diced
¼ cup chopped green chiles, rinsed and drained
¼ cup diced red onion
¼ cup diced green pepper
2 tablespoons chopped fresh parsley
1 tablespoon lime juice
¼ teaspoon cumin
¼ teaspoon hot sauce
⅛ teaspoon salt
⅛ teaspoon garlic powder

Combine all ingredients in a bowl, mixing well; let stand 15 minutes to blend flavors. Serve with unsalted tortilla chips or with grilled chicken or fish. Yield: 3 cups. Serving size: 1 tablespoon (3 calories per serving).

PROTEIN 0.1 / FAT 0.0 / CARBOHYDRATE 0.6 / FIBER 0.1 / CHOLESTEROL 0 / SODIUM 8 / POTASSIUM 23

TEXAS MOPPING SAUCE

½ cup reduced-calorie catsup
3 tablespoons dark corn syrup
2 tablespoons lemon juice
2 tablespoons Worcestershire sauce
2 teaspoons instant coffee granules
2 teaspoons liquid smoke

Combine all ingredients in a small bowl, stirring well. Use as a basting sauce for brisket, beef, or chicken. Yield: ¾ cup plus 2 tablespoons (19 calories per tablespoon).

PROTEIN 0.1 / FAT 0.0 / CARBOHYDRATE 4.6 / CHOLESTEROL 0 / IRON 0.2 / SODIUM 26 / CALCIUM 5

PICANTE MARINADE

1 (8-ounce) can tomato sauce
2 tablespoons vegetable oil
1 tablespoon liquid jalapeño sauce
2 teaspoons sugar
2 teaspoons vinegar
1 large clove garlic, crushed

Combine all ingredients in a saucepan; cook over medium heat until thoroughly heated. Use to marinate chicken, beef, or pork. Marinate meat in refrigerator several hours or overnight. Baste with remaining marinade during cooking. Yield: 1 cup (22 calories per tablespoon).

PROTEIN 0.2 / FAT 1.8 / CARBOHYDRATE 1.7 / CHOLESTEROL 0 / IRON 0.1 / SODIUM 93 / CALCIUM 2

DESSERTS

FLAMING KAHLÚA FLAN

---

2 tablespoons dark brown sugar
4 eggs
¼ cup sugar
¼ cup Kahlúa or other coffee-flavored liqueur, divided
½ teaspoon vanilla extract
2 cups skim milk

Sprinkle brown sugar in bottom of a 4-cup ring mold; set aside.

Beat eggs at medium speed of an electric mixer until frothy. Add sugar, 2 tablespoons Kahlúa, and vanilla; beat just until blended. Add skim milk; beat well. Pour mixture into prepared mold. Place in a 13-× 9-× 2-inch baking dish. Pour 1 inch of hot water into baking dish. Bake at 300° for 55 minutes or until a knife inserted near edge comes out clean. Remove mold from water; let cool on a wire rack 20 minutes.

Loosen edges of flan with a knife. Invert onto a serving platter.

Place remaining 2 tablespoons Kahlúa in a small, long-handled saucepan; heat just until warm (do not boil). Remove from heat. Ignite with a long match; pour over flan. Serve when flames die down. Yield: 8 servings (94 calories per serving).

PROTEIN 5.2 / FAT 2.9 / CARBOHYDRATE 15.2 / CHOLESTEROL 138 / IRON 0.6 / SODIUM 67 / CALCIUM 91

KAHLÚA CRÈME CUSTARDS

¼ cup ground chocolate-flavored coffee beans
2 cups skim milk, scalded
3 eggs
3 tablespoons firmly packed brown sugar
2 teaspoons Kahlúa or other coffee-flavored liqueur
Vegetable cooking spray
2 tablespoons Kahlúa or other coffee-flavored liqueur,
    divided

Place a coffee filter in a large strainer; place strainer over a medium bowl. Spoon ground coffee into filter. Pour hot milk over coffee; set aside until all of the milk has dripped through.

Combine eggs, brown sugar, and 2 teaspoons Kahlúa in a medium bowl; beat at high speed of an electric mixer until well blended. Gradually add reserved milk mixture, beating constantly. Spoon mixture into six (6-ounce) custard cups coated with cooking spray.

Place custard cups in a 13- × 9- × 2-inch baking dish; pour hot water into baking dish to a depth of 1 inch. Bake at 325° for 40 minutes or until a knife inserted halfway between center and edge of custard comes out clean. Remove cups from water; cool to room temperature. Chill thoroughly. Turn custard out onto individual serving plates; spoon 1 teaspoon Kahlúa over each. Serve immediately. Yield: 6 servings (116 calories per serving).

PROTEIN 5.9 / FAT 2.9 / CARBOHYDRATE 12.9 / FIBER 0.0 / CHOLESTEROL 139 / SODIUM 79 / POTASSIUM 245

CINNAMON SPICE CAKE

Vegetable cooking spray
¾ cup plus 2 tablespoons cake flour
1 teaspoon baking powder
½ teaspoon ground cinnamon
½ teaspoon ground nutmeg
¼ teaspoon ground cloves
¼ cup margarine, softened
⅓ cup sugar
¼ cup skim milk
1 egg
½ teaspoon vanilla extract
1 tablespoon powdered sugar

Coat an 8-inch square pan with cooking spray; set aside.

Combine cake flour and next 4 ingredients; stir well, and set aside.

Cream margarine; gradually add ⅓ cup sugar, beating well at medium speed of an electric mixer. Add flour mixture, and beat well. Combine milk, egg, and vanilla; add to creamed mixture. Beat at low speed of electric mixer until blended. Continue beating mixture at high speed 2 minutes.

Pour batter into prepared pan. Bake at 350° for 25 to 30 minutes or until wooden pick inserted in center comes out clean. Let cool. Sift powdered sugar over cooled cake. Yield: 9 servings (134 calories per serving).

PROTEIN 2.0 / FAT 5.8 / CARBOHYDRATE 18.5 / CHOLESTEROL 22 / IRON 1.1 / SODIUM 104 / CALCIUM 38

RUM COMPOTE IN TORTILLA SHELLS

1 cup sliced, peeled fresh peaches
1 cup sliced plums
1 cup honeydew melon chunks
1 cup fresh pineapple chunks
1 tablespoon sugar
2 tablespoons rum
½ teaspoon grated lemon rind
1 tablespoon lemon juice
6 (6-inch) flour tortillas
2 tablespoons sugar
½ teaspoon ground cinnamon
2 tablespoons margarine, melted and divided

Combine first 8 ingredients in a medium bowl; toss lightly. Cover and refrigerate 2 hours.

Stack tortillas, and wrap in aluminum foil; bake at 350° for 7 minutes to soften. Set aside, and keep warm.

Combine 2 tablespoons sugar and cinnamon, stirring well. Brush one side of each tortilla with ½ teaspoon melted margarine; sprinkle with ½ teaspoon sugar-cinnamon mixture. Turn tortillas over, and repeat procedure on other side. Place tortillas in each of six 10-ounce custard cups; gently place a 6-ounce custard cup in center of each tortilla, shaping tortilla into a bowl. Bake at 475° for 5 minutes; remove tortillas from custard cups, and place on cookie sheet. Bake an additional 5 minutes or until lightly browned and crisp. Remove tortillas to wire racks, and cool completely.

Place tortilla shells on individual serving plates. Drain fruit, discarding liquid. Spoon fruit into shells; serve immediately. Yield: 6 servings (232 calories per serving).

PROTEIN 3.1 / FAT 5.8 / CARBOHYDRATE 41.8 / FIBER 2.5 / CHOLESTEROL 0 / SODIUM 51 / POTASSIUM 241